STEALING HOME
THE STORY OF JACKIE ROBINSON

Also by Barry Denenberg

An American Hero:
The True Story of Charles A. Lindbergh

When Will This Cruel War Be Over? The Civil War Diary
of Emma Simpson

Voices from Vietnam

The True Story of J. Edgar Hoover and the FBI

Nelson Mandela: "No Easy Walk to Freedom"

John Fitzgerald Kennedy: America's 35th President

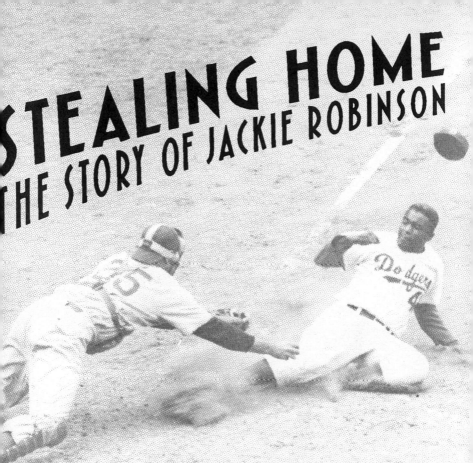

STEALING HOME
THE STORY OF JACKIE ROBINSON

BARRY DENENBERG

SCHOLASTIC INC.
New York Toronto London Auckland Sydney
Mexico City New Delhi Hong Kong Buenos Aires

Photo Credits

Frontis: UPI; 2: New York Public Library; 5: courtesy of the Robinson family; 11: National Archives; 18 & 19: Wide World; 22: Metromedia L.A.; 27: National Baseball Library; 35 & 39: Wide World; 46: Culver Pictures; 61: UPI; 68: Magnum; 73 & 76: Wide World; 78: International News Photos; 88: UPI; 89: Brooklyn National League; 90 & 91: UPI; 97: Wide World; 99: National Baseball Library; 106: National Conference of Christians and Jews; 108 & 112: Wide World; 115: UPI; 117: UPI

ISBN-13: 978-0-590-42560-5
ISBN-10: 0-590-42560-9

Copyright © 1990 by Barry Denenberg.
All rights reserved. Published by Scholastic Inc.
SCHOLASTIC and associated logos are trademarks
and/or registered trademarks of Scholastic Inc.

60 59 58 57 56 55 54   14 15 16/0

Printed in the U.S.A.

First Scholastic printing, May 1990

To Kaicho Nakamura, my instructors,
and fellow students at Seido Karate

A life is not important except in the impact it has on other lives.

— Jackie Robinson

1
California Childhood

Jack Roosevelt Robinson was born on a farm near Cairo, Georgia, on January 31, 1919. The Robinsons lived on part of a farm owned by somebody else. The owner of the farm gave Mallie Robinson and her husband a horse, a plow, feed for animals, and some other equipment. They had to repay him by giving him half of whatever they grew. Mallie's father had been a slave, and although this wasn't slavery, it wasn't far from it. It was called sharecropping and was a lot of work for little reward.

When Jackie was only six months old his father left and never came back. He told his wife he was going to visit his brother in Texas. Mallie never heard from him again.

Sharecroppers' cabins in Georgia during the early part of this century

Jackie was the baby of the family. His brother Edgar, born in 1910, was the oldest. Then came Frank, who was born in 1912; Matthew, called "Mack," who arrived two years later; and Willa Mae, Jackie's only sister, who was three years older than he. From the day he was born Jackie was his mother's favorite — and no one seemed to mind.

With her husband gone and five small children to take care of, Mallie Robinson simply could not get all the work done. The owner of the farm was happy to get rid of her. He was angry that she hadn't warned him that Mr. Robinson was going to run off. If he had known, he told her, he would have had the sheriff stop him. Mrs. Robinson said, "Slavery's over, Mr. Sasser, and that man is free to go where he pleases." "You're too uppity for your own good," Sasser told her. ("Uppity" was what some southern white people called black people who didn't do exactly what they were told.) Mallie was forced to take her children to live temporarily with a family she had worked for before she got married.

The next spring Mallie decided to join her brother in Southern California. He had settled there after he returned from fighting in World War I. Mallie was excited about starting over in California. When she was a child she had heard stories about what it was like to be a slave. She wanted her family to be as far away from that kind of life as possible. She wanted her children to have a better chance in life than she had.

The Robinsons lived in a small three-room apartment when they first arrived in Pasadena, California. Mallie's brother lived there, along with her sister, her sister's husband, and their two children. They all slept in one room and Jackie's brothers and sister in another. Jackie stayed with his mother in her room. There was no hot water and no sink. A big tin tub where the dishes were washed stood in the kitchen. It was also used for baths.

Mallie found work cooking, cleaning, washing, and ironing for a white family in Pasadena. Since the Robinsons were so poor she also received money from the government. Somehow, by 1923 she had saved enough money to place a down payment on a small corner house at 121 Pepper Street.

The Robinsons were the only black family in the area. Their white neighbors gave them a hard time as soon as they'd moved in. Once the police came because someone had complained that Edgar's roller skates were too noisy. Their neighbors not only bothered the Robinsons in small ways, but they even considered buying the house back from Mallie, although that plan fell through. Jackie and his brothers also got into plenty of fights with the white kids on their block.

Jackie Robinson and his family. From left: Mack, Jackie, Edgar, Mallie Robinson (seated), Willa Mae, and Frank

Mallie often had to leave for work before the children were up. When Jackie was still too young to go to school, and there was no one to take care of him, his mother decided that Willa Mae should take him to school with her. He could play in the sandbox until his sister got out for the day. That way she would be able to keep an eye on him.

Willa Mae returned from her first day in kindergarten with a note from her teacher. He didn't want her to bring her brother to school anymore. Mallie wouldn't give up. That night she taught Jackie to say "Good morning, teacher," and in the morning she sent the two of them off again. The teacher still didn't approve. Mallie went to see him. She explained her problem. She *had* to work or the family wouldn't have a roof over their heads or food on their table. She couldn't leave little Jackie home alone. She knew that leaving him in the sandbox wasn't the best idea in the world but she didn't know what else to do. The teacher was impressed with how responsible Willa Mae was. And he sympathized with Mallie. Jackie returned to his sandbox.

Jackie's first school was Grover Cleveland School — the one with the sandbox. He behaved himself but didn't do too well in class. His mind was on something else — playing games outside.

Because of his brothers and sisters, who were

all good athletes, Jackie always played with kids older than he was. They might have been bigger, but he was quicker. Even his mother helped Jackie play the games he loved. At one point she unraveled some old woolen socks and wound the yarn into a ball. Then she covered it with a rag, tied it tight, and sent Jackie into the street. He picked up the first good stick he found and was on his way.

The kids at school always wanted Jackie on their teams. They would offer him bribes — part of their lunches, or even money. Having Jackie on your side assured victory, no matter what sport was being played.

After school the kids would play marbles, tag, or softball in a nearby vacant lot. Or they'd roller skate and zoom around on homemade wagons with wheels nailed on.

When Jackie wasn't playing with his friends he was thinking of ways to make money. He and his brothers and Willa Mae contributed all they could to help their mother. This was the time of the Great Depression. Since the stock market crash of 1929, the United States and the rest of the world had fallen into an economic depression. Millions of people found themselves out of work. Businesses failed and so did banks, sometimes wiping out a family's entire life savings. All across America people were doing whatever they could to scrape by. Many were penniless and dependent on the government for food and shelter. Mallie was fortunate that she was able to keep her job and had children who could help her shoulder the burden.

Jackie used a little red wagon to collect old newspapers to sell to the junk man. Later, when he was ten, he sold hot dogs at the nearby Rose Bowl stadium. At the end of the day he would race under the empty seats looking for any money that had fallen from people's pockets. Jackie also caddied at one of the private golf courses in the area and got up at four A.M. on Sundays to deliver the newspaper.

When he was in the ninth and tenth grades, Jackie hung out with his friends to see what they could stir up. They were called the Pepper Street Gang. Members were not only white and black, but Japanese and Mexican also. Although they weren't out to do any real harm, they didn't shy away from mischief. One prank they loved was to hide on the gold course waiting for balls to be driven down the fairway. One of them, usually Jackie because he was the quickest, would grab the ball and dart back behind the bushes. They had a good time laughing while the man looked for his ball. Later they sold the balls to the golfers back at the clubhouse.

Mallie felt badly that her children's clothes

were secondhand. Sometimes her employers gave them clothes, and other times Jackie's teachers, seeing how worn his clothes were, brought in a bag of old clothes for him. Although she wasn't home as much as she would like, the path Mallie wanted her children to follow was clearly marked. She taught them that if they worked hard and had faith in God then things would work out. She made sure none of the children missed a Sunday at their Methodist Church, but hard work came first. The Robinson children could see how hard their mother struggled so they could have a better life. She never complained and managed to enjoy what she did have. The children loved their mother, but maybe more importantly they respected her. They all wanted her to be proud of them — especially Jackie.

At George Washington High School Jackie's athletic reputation grew. The older he got the faster and more coordinated he became. He started to develop a fierce competitive edge. His winning spirit spread to the whole team, no matter what sport he played. And he played every sport — even tennis and golf, excelling at those, too. He even won the city Ping-Pong championship. Although softball was Jackie's favorite sport, he was beginning to enjoy playing basketball and football. He also went out for track, just like his brother Mack.

When Jackie was seventeen Mack went to Berlin, Germany, for the 1936 Olympics. Many people feared that there would soon be war between the United States and Germany. Adolf Hitler, who was the dictator of Germany, was attending the Olympic games. Hitler believed that white people, except for Jewish people, were superior in all ways to other races. Hitler came to the Olympics to see his blond, blue-eyed German athletes prove his theory in competition. Things didn't work out as Hitler had hoped. A black athlete from the United States named Jesse Owens performed brilliantly in track. And Mack finished second to Owens, winning a silver medal in the 200 meters.

After leaving George Washington Jackie entered Muir Technical High School. By this time his name was well known in the area. Muir Tech's opponents all wanted to "stop Robinson." It was easier said than done. Jackie won letters in football, basketball, track, and baseball.

At this point Jackie had already decided that his career would be in sports. He had seen the difficulties his brother Mack was encountering. Even though Mack was an Olympic hero, he had been fired from his job at a city pool just because he was black. The only work he could find after that was as a janitor or laborer. And Mack wasn't the only one. Jackie could see that his chances of

The black athlete Jesse Owens shocked Adolf Hitler by winning four gold medals in the 1936 Olympics.

getting ahead in a world run by whites were slim. But professional sports might be a place where he could excel. His athletic gifts combined with his keen competitive nature might enable him to hurdle the obstacles found in the non-sports world. Sports would be the way up for him.

2
An Athlete for All Seasons

When he graduated from high school Jackie decided to go to Pasadena Junior College. His brother Frank was disappointed that Jackie hadn't been offered an athletic scholarship to attend one of the bigger universities. (These scholarships are financial aid given to students who are good athletes but do not have enough money to continue their education.) Frank was like a father to Jackie. As a child Frank was often sick and unable to play sports. He took great pride in Jackie's career. Frank felt Jackie hadn't been offered scholarships because he wasn't the type of black person the big schools wanted. They wanted blacks, who at that time were called Negroes, to be meek — to be obedient and accept whatever came their way. They didn't want blacks who made waves. Jackie already had a reputation as someone who was far from meek. Like his mother, Jackie was called "uppity."

Jackie was excited about his first college football season but broke his ankle in practice and had to sit out the first four games. The team lost all four. When his ankle healed he took over as first-string quarterback and Pasadena didn't lose a game for the rest of the season.

The next year nineteen-year-old Jackie started out on the right foot. He led the Pasadena football team to eleven straight victories, gaining over a thousand yards rushing and scoring seventeen touchdowns. He scored 131 of the team's total of 369 points. He had runs that year of 76 and 83 yards. In one game he himself scored three touchdowns and ran in another for three points. In the last game of the season he ran a kickoff for a 104-yard touchdown.

Jackie was the top scorer on the Pasadena basketball team. As a forward he averaged nineteen points a game and was named to the All-State Team. With Jackie leading the way, his team had one of their best seasons in years. He was the only black player on the starting five.

Some California sports fans couldn't believe Jackie could play so many sports so well. After football and basketball season were over he went out for baseball and track. He ran the 100- and 200-meter dashes and did the broad jump. One day, it looked as if he had tried to do too much. The baseball team was scheduled to play the championship game at the same time the track team was supposed to compete in a conference track meet. Finally a plan was worked out. Jackie was allowed to compete early at the track meet. Officials were there to measure his broad jump attempts. That left him time to try and get to his baseball game. Although his family and friends had wondered if he would be able to concentrate at the track meet, Jackie, not content with just competing, set a new junior college world record for the broad jump — 25 feet, 6 ½ inches. The old record had been set by his brother Mack when he attended Pasadena Junior College.

There wasn't much time to celebrate, though. As soon as he was finished, Jackie was whisked into a car and rushed to the baseball game. It was already the third inning when Jackie took over as shortstop. His team won the game and the championship.

Jackie had a great season. He sparkled as shortstop and tore up the base paths, stealing twenty-five bases in just twenty-four games. He hit .417 and was named the Most Valuable Junior College Player in Southern California.

Scouts from the major universities, who had been hired to search for athletic talent around the country, heard about Jackie and came to take a look. There was even talk that he had the potential to be the best all-around athlete in Southern California history. The scouts liked what they saw and Jackie got lots of offers. Some of the offers were pretty tempting and some were a little shady. One scout offered to give Jackie's girlfriend a scholarship also, if Jackie decided to go to the school the scout represented. Jackie was astounded by the offer, and anyway, he didn't have a girlfriend. Another scout made an even stranger offer. He represented a West Coast college that offered Jackie a scholarship to come to their school. If Jackie didn't accept this scholarship, the scout wanted to make sure he wouldn't play for any of their rivals in California. So they would be willing to pay for his tuition to any *East Coast* school he chose, just as long as Jackie didn't play against their team. Jackie and Frank had a good laugh over that one.

Frank was glad when Jackie decided to stay at home and go to the University of California at Los Angeles. UCLA was located right in Pasadena. Jackie wasn't about to leave his biggest fan. He knew that if he played out of state, Frank would not be able to see him play. Jackie not only wanted to be near Frank and the rest of the family, but he was thinking about his future. He felt it would be easier to get a job after school if he stayed at home and built his reputation there. He was going to study physical education.

Sadly, Frank would never see his brother play at UCLA. In May, 1939, he died in a motorcycle accident. It was a confusing and painful time for Jackie. The memory of those awful days never left him.

Jackie got into trouble as soon as he hit the UCLA campus in the fall of 1939. He was driving with some friends when they were cut off by another car. They chased the car and caught up with it at a stoplight. Everyone got out as people gathered to watch. The situation was so tense that the first policeman on the scene drew his gun and started arresting people. Jackie was charged with blocking the sidewalk and resisting arrest. Later the white driver admitted Jackie hadn't done anything wrong. Nothing much happened after that, but it was a bad beginning. People started talking about how Jackie was a troublemaker. Jackie tried to put it behind him and concentrate on the upcoming football season.

The UCLA football team was not expected to be very good that year. They did, however, have two outstanding players. One was Jackie and the other was Kenny Washington, who was also black. These two All-American halfbacks made it a surprisingly good year for the Bruins of UCLA.

In the second game of the season Jackie had a 65-yard, game-winning touchdown run. Against nationally ranked Stanford, the Bruins were the

Although Jackie Robinson became famous playing baseball, he actually preferred football and starred on UCLA's team.

Jackie was the first four-letter athlete in UCLA's history.

underdogs. But Jackie made an interception late in the fourth quarter, and the Bruins drove in for a touchdown. Jackie kicked the point after, for a tie. After this upset the Stanford coach said that Jackie was "the greatest backfield runner I have seen [in] twenty-five years." It was a special game for Jackie because it was played at the Rose Bowl, near where he grew up.

Thanks to Robinson and Washington the UCLA team had hopes of playing in the post-season Rose Bowl game. But first they had to beat the Trojans of the University of Southern California. Jackie made a desperate attempt to catch a pass in the end zone at the end of the game. But he couldn't come up with it, and the game ended in a scoreless tie.

The USC Trojans had a better record, and they went on to play in the Rose Bowl game. Jackie was disappointed even though he had had a great year. He was the nation's leading ball carrier, averaging 12 yards per carry. On punt returns he averaged 21 yards per kick.

During Jackie's second year Kenny Washington graduated, and the opposition football teams were able to concentrate on stopping Jackie, making it a frustrating football season for him. Basketball was another story. He was the star of the team and led the Pacific Coast conference in scoring for two years. In his second year he was named to the All-Division team. The University of California coach called Jackie the best college basketball player in the country.

Jackie continued competing in the broad jump as a member of the track team. In his first year he won the National Collegiate Championship. Oddly enough Jackie's worst sport was baseball. The UCLA team wasn't very good and Jackie batted only .200. In his first game, however, he managed to steal five bases, stealing home twice.

But Jackie's senior year at UCLA was exciting because of something having nothing to do with sports.

One day friends introduced him to a pretty girl named Rachel Isum. Rachel had heard about the tall, good-looking campus sports hero. But she had always stayed away from "jocks." In her opinion they were too stuck-up. Rachel had to admit, though, that Jackie was very polite, which she hadn't expected, and had a good sense of humor. Most surprising he seemed shy. He didn't act like the Big-Man-On-Campus type. And he was handsome.

Jackie knew his way around the athletic field, but when it came to girls, he was strictly an amateur. Plenty of girls wanted to meet him, but he felt that was just because he had caught a game-winning touchdown pass or scored a crucial basket. Jackie didn't want that kind of attention. He

Like his brother Mack, a silver-medal-winner in the 1936 Olympics, Jackie was a track star.

was interested in more down-to-earth girls. He wanted someone who was serious the way he was. His reputation was that he was a "lone wolf" — keeping to himself most of the time. He was so cautious that Rachel realized she would have to make the first move. She did her best to be wherever he might turn up, although she tried not to be too obvious about it. Thanks to her efforts they talked quite a few times. Finally Jackie asked her to be his date for the Homecoming Dance. She accepted and they began seeing each other "seriously."

Four months later Jackie surprised Rachel with the news that he was quitting school. He said he wanted to get a job and earn money so that he could help his mother. He felt that Mallie had worked long and hard enough and it was time she was able to rest. He had been offered a job at a youth camp and was pretty sure that it could lead to an even better job as athletic director of a new youth camp planned by the same organization. Jackie was very excited about the opportunity and took the job. While Rachel sympathized with his concern for his mother, she told him it seemed a shame to leave school so close to graduation. Yet Jackie's mind was made up.

The news that Jackie Robinson was leaving UCLA was all over the sports pages. The newspapers said he was:

*the best all-around athlete ever to play on the West Coast
*the best all-around athlete in America
*the best black athlete of all time

He became the first athlete in UCLA history to earn major letters in four different sports in one year: baseball, football, basketball, and track.

3
Black Soldier

Jackie liked his job at the youth camp. He enjoyed working with the kids and hoped that what he was teaching would help keep them out of trouble. But the job didn't pay well and Jackie had to think of other ways to make money. He would have liked to play professional football, but that was out of the question in 1941. A black athlete had played for the Eagles in 1933 but no other black players had since. In the fall of 1941 Jackie joined the L.A. Bulldogs, an all-black football team that traveled around the country playing opponents wherever they could find them. After that he went to Hawaii where he was a big attraction with the Honolulu Bears.

When the football season ended he stayed in

Hawaii and worked as a laborer. He left, bound for the mainland, on December 5, 1941. Two days later, on December 7, 1941, 360 Japanese bombers attacked the U.S. Pacific Fleet at Pearl Harbor. The United States now entered World War II.

Because of the broken ankle he had suffered back in junior college, Jackie went into the army with a limited service status. In April, 1942, he was sent to Fort Riley, Kansas, for basic training. Jackie wanted to be an officer so he applied to Officer's Candidate School. He was told, off the record, that blacks weren't welcomed at OCS. Around that time Joe Louis, the popular, black heavyweight boxing champion, was transferred to Fort Riley. Jackie and Joe played golf together, and the champ agreed to help him. He made some calls to influential friends, and soon Jackie and other blacks were allowed into OCS. In January, 1943, Jackie was awarded the rank of lieutenant. He was twenty-four years old. To celebrate he bought an engagement ring for Rae (Rachel's nickname). Writing to Rae was the highlight of Jackie's social life in the army and he wrote almost every day. Rae was studying nursing in San Francisco during the day and working as a riveter in an aircraft factory at night.

World War II changed things for people all over the world. In the United States the relationship between black people and white people began to change. At that time the army was segregated:

26

With the help of Joe Louis, the famous boxer, Jackie was admitted to Officers' Candidate School and became a lieutenant in the U.S. Army.

Black soldiers were separated from white soldiers. Black soldiers began asking themselves a lot of questions. Why were they going to fight a war against Hitler when they weren't treated like equals in America, their own home? Some blacks didn't want to fight. Others wanted to fight to show they were just as good as whites, and just as patriotic. It was a heated and important debate, and Jackie found himself right in the middle. He hated the segregated conditions in the army. "I was in two wars, one against a foreign enemy, the other against prejudice at home."

Jackie grew more and more disturbed by the treatment black soldiers were given at Fort Riley. Finally he had seen enough and felt he had to do something. He phoned a Major Hafner and told him about his complaints. It was a long and unpleasant conversation. Major Hafner didn't like the conversation from the beginning. He decided to be more direct with Lieutenant Robinson. Since the two were talking on the phone, Major Hafner hadn't realized that Lieutenant Robinson was black. He said, "Well, Lieutenant Robinson. Let me put it to you this way: How would you like to have your wife sitting next to a nigger?" The conversation ended shortly after that.

That was Jackie's first major run-in with racism in the army. And it wasn't going to be his last. When he had first arrived at Fort Riley, he had tried to play on the baseball team. The captain threatened to break up the team if he had to play with a black man. Jackie never played an inning.

Football, however, was another story. In the senseless world of army segregation, it was okay for blacks to play football. The officers, knowing Jackie's reputation, wanted him on their team. Jackie knew he couldn't refuse, but he made it plain he wouldn't be trying very hard if they forced him to play.

His decision was not a popular one at Fort Riley. Jackie said: "If I'm good enough for football then I'm good enough for baseball. And if I'm good enough for those, then I'm good enough to sit where I want, eat where I want, and go to the latrine where and when I want." Jackie was soon transferred to Camp Hood, Texas. The white officers at Fort Riley had heard enough from the outspoken Lieutenant Robinson.

Things went pretty well at Camp Hood until one summer night. Jackie was coming back to camp. He had been at the hospital having his ankle looked at and was traveling with the wife of a fellow black officer. The woman was light-skinned, and the bus driver assumed Jackie was sitting next to a white woman. This was not allowed in many states, including Texas. The driver wanted Jackie to go to the back of the bus, where blacks were required to sit. Jackie had no intention of moving. The driver threatened Jackie, who looked up at him and said, "I don't care what kind of trouble you plan to cause me. You can't cause me any trouble I haven't already faced. . . . I don't intend to go to the back of the bus. So get out of my face and go drive the bus. . . ."

At the last stop Jackie was confronted by the dispatcher and two other drivers. He was not about to be pushed around by them, either. "Listen, buddy," he said with his finger pointed in the dispatcher's face, "let's get a couple of things straight. You're a civilian and your job is to run the bus system. The army decides policies on the post, and a ruling just came down from Washington that there will be no more bus segregation on army posts. . . ."

By now the military police had arrived. Jackie still refused to back down. He was told that charges would be filed against him. Two weeks later Jackie was told he would have to stand trial for disobeying military orders.

Jackie's case was talked about as another example of the kind of mistreatment that was bothering black soldiers. Jackie was very angry about the situation. He felt he had done nothing wrong but still had to defend himself. All he had been doing was taking a bus ride.

Many blacks were offering Jackie whatever help they could. A group of black officers asked the National Association for the Advancement of

Colored People (the NAACP) to get involved. Writers from two of the country's larger black newspapers also offered to help. They were able to get the charges reduced. Jackie was now accused only of being disrespectful to a superior officer. It was said that he gave sloppy salutes and was rude. "Having received a lawful command from [the] Captain, [Lieutenant Robinson] did . . . willfully disobey . . ."

On August 2, 1944, Jackie's military trial began. Jackie's own superior officer spoke very highly of him. His sincerity and admiration for Jackie was obvious. The testimony against Jackie was well rehearsed and untrue. Jackie's lawyer, summing up the case, said that this was "simply a situation in which a few individuals sought to vent their bigotry on a Negro they considered 'uppity' because he had the audacity to seek to exercise rights that belonged to him as an American and a soldier." Jackie was cleared of all charges against him.

By now Jackie had had enough of the army and the feeling was mutual. He applied for a medical discharge because of the bone chips in his ankle. In November, 1944, his honorable discharge came through. Jackie Robinson was a civilian once again.

4
Only the Ball Was White

Jackie didn't really give too much thought to playing baseball. If he was going to be a professional athlete, it would be on the football field, not the baseball diamond — and it didn't much matter because he was planning a career as a coach or athletic director. But one day, just before he was discharged from the army, he was walking past some guys playing baseball. They hit a foul ball Jackie's way. Instinctively he reached down, scooped up the ball, and threw a strike to one of the players. The player turned out to be a pitcher with the Kansas City Monarchs of the Negro American League. He was impressed with how cleanly Jackie fielded the ball and the accuracy of his arm. He told Jackie that the Monarchs were always on the lookout for good players and suggested Jackie contact them. The money was good, and the conversation remained in the back of Jackie's mind.

In January, 1945, after he was discharged, Jackie took a job as basketball coach at Sam Houston College, a small black school in Texas. The job turned out to be a disappointment and the pay was low. He wrote a letter to the Kansas City Monarchs. The Monarchs had heard of Jackie from his California college days. By April, 1945, Jackie had accepted their offer of $400 a month to play professional baseball.

Rachel was not happy with the news. Jackie would be traveling a lot. He would be away almost all the time. Jackie told her not to worry. Playing baseball was just something temporary. One hundred dollars a week was good pay, and he could give most of it to his mother. Then, as soon as he made enough, he would quit and get something permanent, something that didn't involve that kind of traveling. Rachel was worrying over nothing — he wasn't about to become a full-time professional baseball player.

The Monarchs' spring training camp was in Houston, Texas. Shortly after Jackie arrived, he was contacted by a writer from a black newspaper. The writer wanted Jackie to join two other black players for a tryout with the Boston Red Sox. Jackie was suspicious, knowing there were no black players in the major leagues. As it turned out, the Red Sox management had been pressured into the tryout by a local, liberal, white politician. They were doing it just to get it over with and had no intention of signing up black ballplayers. When the three players arrived in Boston they were told that the tryout was postponed a day. The next day they heard the same thing. This went on for four days. By the time they ran on to the field at Boston's Fenway Park, they knew this tryout wasn't for real. The Red Sox went through the motions, but none of the players expected to hear from them. And they never did.

In 1945, when Jackie Robinson joined the Kansas City Monarchs, major league baseball was a white man's game. It had been that way ever since organized baseball began in 1869. Organized baseball meant: official leagues and teams, schedules that could be depended on, and players' contracts and salaries. Blacks were not allowed to play in organized baseball, which was to become today's American and National Leagues. Any team that had a black player wasn't allowed in the league and that was the end of that.

Eventually black athletes formed their own teams and their own leagues. In 1920 the Negro National League was founded, and seventeen years later the Negro American League was es-

Jackie Robinson played for the Kansas City Monarchs of the Negro American League.

tablished. The first all-black baseball team was called the Cuban Giants. They called themselves Cuban, even though they were all black Americans, because they wanted to be able to play against white teams. Cubans could play against white teams but blacks couldn't. To make sure no one suspected anything they pretended they were speaking Spanish when they were on the field. Although none of it made sense in any language, it seemed to work.

Black teams traveled around the country playing anyone they could find. This was called "barnstorming." Black baseball was responsible for many innovations. The modern day "squeezer" type of catcher's mitt originated in black baseball because base stealing was a bigger part of the game in the Negro Leagues, and getting the ball out of the glove quickly was essential. Black catchers had kept removing the padding from the "pillow" type of catcher's mitt until they had the minimum amount they needed to keep the glove flexible and allow them to grab the ball and throw out would-be base stealers. Black umpires were the first to wear chest protectors inside their coats so that they could get a closer look at the pitch. Batting helmets, which were originally just workmen's hard hats, first made their debut in black baseball.

Perhaps the most important innovation introduced by black baseball was the introduction of night games. It was important that the teams play as many games as possible to keep the money coming in. Sometimes a team arrived in a town after sundown, so the players figured out a way to play at night. In 1929 the Kansas City Monarchs were the first to play under lights. They traveled with their own lighting system. When they arrived in a town they installed the lights on poles all around the field. A big dynamo was placed in the outfield to generate the electricity. When the game was over, they took everything apart, loaded up the bus, and set off for the next town. (The first night game in the major leagues wasn't until a 1935 Cincinnati Reds game.)

Sometimes Negro League teams played three games in a day. Pitchers pitched both ends of a doubleheader — hurling two complete games. Many times the teams slept on the bus; they were rarely in the same city for more than a day. Black teams traveled almost all the time, and not only across the United States. In the spring and summer they played other black clubs and some semi-pro white teams. But in the winter it was too cold to play in the U.S., so they went south to Cuba, South and Central America, Mexico, and the Caribbean.

Some black players developed national reputations, even though their names were never mentioned in white newspapers. Josh Gibson was a home run hitter known as the "Babe Ruth of black baseball." It was said that "Cool Papa" Bell was so fast "he could turn off the light in his hotel room and be asleep before it got dark." Satchel Paige became a legend. He was such a good pitcher that if a batter fouled off a pitch or two they said that Satchel didn't have his stuff that day. After striking out against Satchel, one hitter was walking back to the dugout. The on-deck batter asked him what Paige was throwing. "I don't know," the batter said, "I didn't see it."

A few white fans in segregated America had heard about Paige or Bell or Gibson. Later, in the 1950s, many of the players from the Negro Leagues would become the stars of the major leagues. One, nicknamed "Pork Chops" because that's all he ate on the road, became known simply as Henry Aaron. In 1974 he would break Babe Ruth's record for hitting the most home runs.

The Commissioner of Baseball from 1920 to 1944 was a former judge named Kenesaw Mountain Landis. One of his first decisions was to stop major league white teams from playing against black teams. He was very powerful and was strongly against letting blacks play in the majors. In 1944 he died and was succeeded by Albert Chandler, whose nickname was "Happy."

By the time Happy Chandler took over, things had started to change. Many of these changes were because of World War II. Both around the world and in America, soldiers returned from the

The great pitcher Satchel Paige was only able to play major-league baseball at the end of his career.

war with different views. Many white and black American soldiers came home with a different attitude toward each other. Blacks would no longer accept being treated as second-class citizens. They were tired of being considered only good enough to be shoeshine boys, train porters, and servants — but not much else. Blacks had fought just as bravely as whites. And they had died leaving their families just as heartbroken. A caption below a photograph of a dead black World War II soldier read:

GOOD ENOUGH TO DIE FOR HIS COUNTRY, BUT NOT GOOD ENOUGH FOR BASEBALL.

The time of baseball being a game for whites only was coming to an end. Sportswriters were writing about the injustice of not allowing blacks to play organized baseball in a country that prided itself on being a democracy.

Jackie's tryout with the Boston Red Sox had been a good sign. Other major league teams were being pressured to sign up black ballplayers. After years of not being talked about, the issue was now being hotly debated: Did blacks belong in major league baseball? Some people said no. Blacks weren't good enough. Some said no, they were too good. If they played there wouldn't be any room left for white players. Some said no because it would cause violence and bloodshed. Anti-black white players would try and drive black players out. They would use their spikes when sliding and would throw at black players' heads when they came to bat. Some said no because they said that black players didn't *want* to play with white players. They said that blacks were more comfortable playing with "their own kind," and anyway, why change things?

But there were others across the country who felt that segregation in the major leagues had gone on long enough. It was time for some of the fine black players from the Negro Leagues to play with white ball players. That way major league baseball could truly be what it was supposed to be: the best competing against the best, regardless of the color of their skin.

Economics played an important role in the attitude toward segregated baseball. The Negro League teams played many of their games in stadiums owned by the white major league teams. When the white teams were out of town, the owner rented the stadiums to the black teams. This was especially true in the big cities of the northeast: New York, Boston, and Philadelphia. The New York Yankees received more than $100,000 a year in rental money from black teams. The white owners were afraid that if blacks were allowed to play in the major leagues, the Negro Leagues would fold. Then the stadiums

41

would lose all their rental money. The black owners of teams in the Negro Leagues were also worried about money. If blacks could play in the majors, they would go out of business.

But none of this could stand in the way of the changes that were slowly coming.

After he was named Commissioner, Happy Chandler made it clear where he stood on the issue of race and baseball: ". . . if a black boy can make it at Okinawa and go to Guadalcanal [two important World War II battles], he can make it in baseball."

Jackie played his first game for the Monarchs without even practicing. After only a few days, he found himself traveling all over the country. It seemed the Monarchs were always on the move, and Jackie found it hard to get used to. He didn't smoke or drink and didn't join in the rowdy life of the road. He wrote to Rachel every day. Traveling through the segregated South was particularly difficult for Jackie to accept. He was not used to drinking fountains that were only for white people or black people. Nor did he take to the fact that most hotels wouldn't allow blacks to stay in them, and that roadside restaurants often refused to feed them. By the end of the season, Jackie had traveled over 30,000 miles.

Jackie did not like playing in the Negro Leagues. The sloppy schedules and the frantic pace annoyed him. Most of the players were southerners, and Jackie just didn't fit in. A number of times he came close to quitting. At the end of his first year he wrote an article for a national magazine. The article was called "What's Wrong with Negro Baseball." He said he considered it a "miserable way to make a buck."

Jackie still managed to have a pretty good year. He hit .345 and was named the starting shortstop for the West in the All-Star Game. But the end of the season found him unsure of his future. He liked playing baseball and felt he could get better. But he didn't like traveling and he didn't like being away from Rachel. Traveling in the segregated South was keeping him in a constant state of anger. He wasn't sure what he would do.

5
Branch Rickey

Branch Rickey was born in Ohio, in 1881 — thirty-eight years before Jackie Robinson. He played semi-pro football and baseball while he was in college so he could pay for his education. He was very religious and would never play on Sundays. Even though he studied to be a lawyer, he always seemed to be more involved in sports.

When Rickey was twenty-four he played baseball for the St. Louis Browns. But he had health problems and had to stop playing. He continued working with the Browns as a coach and a scout. In 1913, when the Browns were in last place, he took over as manager. The next year they finished fifth.

Four years later Rickey took over as manager of the other St. Louis team, the Cardinals. This time he took the last-place Cardinals to third place. Branch Rickey invented the "farm system," a network of minor league teams that would assure the Cardinals of getting young ballplayers as they developed.

In 1926 (when Jackie was seven years old), Rickey's Cardinals won the World Series for the first time since 1888. He was with them for the next seventeen years. During that time they became one of the most feared teams in baseball history. His most famous Cardinal team was known as the "Gashouse Gang." They were feisty and fearless and would do anything to win. They got into almost as many fights with each other as they did with their opponents.

By 1942, however, Rickey was having serious conflicts with the owner of the team. That year the Cardinals won the most games they had ever won. Some people said their farm teams were as good as most major league clubs. They won another World Series that year, but Rickey and the owner just didn't get along. Rickey had to go. He had been with the Cardinals for twenty-five years and was baseball's highest paid executive.

Sixty-one-year-old Branch Rickey now became the general manager (GM) of the Brooklyn Dodgers. (The Dodgers were named that because it was

Branch Rickey, the man who would integrate baseball

said that to survive in Brooklyn you had to be able to dodge the electrified streetcars that were everywhere.) He didn't waste any time building the Dodgers into a powerful team. The first order of business was finding talent. Talent for the present *and* the future. Mr. Rickey, as he was now called, developed an elaborate scouting system. He hired men who knew their business and whose opinions he trusted. His scouts were scattered across America.

He sent 20,000 letters to high school coaches asking them to recommend talented young players. He doubled the amount of scouts he first employed and then doubled them again. He signed over 400 players to contracts. Most of them were young and inexperienced, but they all had potential.

Rickey traveled around the country looking for new young talent. He was one of the master traders in baseball history. After a trade the other general manager often wondered how Rickey had gotten away with it.

Rickey kept an elaborate index-card filing system. It contained the names of all the high school and college players he wanted to keep tabs on. He hired a statistician to chart pitches. The Dodger farm system became second to none. Branch Rickey made it clear to anyone who cared to listen that he would do whatever it took to put together a winning team. And if that meant signing up a black player then that is what he would do:

> [A black] *player or two will not only help the Brooklyn Organization — but putting colored players in the major leagues will also accomplish something that is long overdue. It is something I have thought about and believed in for a long time.*

Rickey *had* been thinking about it for a long time. At least as far back as when he was a baseball coach at Ohio-Wesleyan University, before he joined the Cardinals. One spring the team traveled to South Bend, Indiana, for a game. When they went to check into their hotel, the desk clerk told Rickey that Charles Thomas, a black player, could not stay there. The hotel was for whites only. Charles Thomas was not only one of the best players on the team, but a fine young man. Rickey was outraged. He argued with the clerk, but it did no good. Thomas volunteered to return home, because he didn't want to cause the team any problems. Rickey told him no. He insisted on seeing the manager of the hotel. He told him he wanted Thomas to stay in his room. Would they be willing to bring up a cot so he could do that? The manager agreed and finally they went up to their room. Charles Thomas sat on the bed and cried, rubbing his hands and saying to his coach: "Black skin, black skin. If only I could make them white."

Branch Rickey never forgot Charles Thomas. He promised himself that he would do whatever he could to see to it that something like this didn't happen again. "I can't do something about racial bigotry in every field, but I can certainly do something about it in baseball."

Branch Rickey was wrong. He *could* do something about racial bigotry in every field — just by doing something about it in baseball. Destiny was about to introduce Branch Rickey and Jackie Robinson, and baseball would never be the same. Neither would life in America.

6
The Meeting

During the 1943 baseball season Branch Rickey announced to the baseball world that his far-reaching scouting system just *might* come up with the name of a qualified black ballplayer. And that he just *might* sign him up. Rickey made it sound like it would be an accident — something that couldn't be avoided. But he was hiding the truth. He had already decided to find the best black ballplayer in the country. Rickey was then going to sign him and make him the first black to play major league baseball.

Rickey was doing it for two simple reasons. Simple, at least, to him. First, he felt it was time to start doing what was right. And second, he thought it would help the Dodgers win the pennant. He was right on both counts.

He told none of his scouts his real plans. He told them he was going to form another, better league for black players: The United States League. The scouts were ordered to look for players for the Dodger team: The Brooklyn Brown Dodgers.

Rickey wanted a player who could run well, had a good throwing arm, and could hit with power. But that was only part of what Rickey was looking for. He was equally concerned about the player's personality, background, intelligence, and desire to succeed. Just being the best baseball player wasn't good enough. Rickey knew what the man would have to put up with. He didn't want someone who was so hot-headed he might punch someone in the nose right away — even if the other guy deserved it. But Rickey also needed someone with enough drive and determination to manage to hold his head up high in spite of the abuse.

Rickey needed someone who could play ball *and* take the heat. Someone who wouldn't fold under the pressure from the fans, the sportswriters, opposing players, and his own teammates. The first black player in organized baseball needed plenty of self-control. He had to avoid reacting to his tormentors. As if all this wasn't enough, Rickey also wanted someone who would set a good example off the field. A non-smoker and a non-drinker. A family man, he hoped, with a college education.

There were many players in the Negro Leagues who were considered good enough to play in the major leagues. Most, however, had to be crossed off the list for one reason or another. Some were simply too old. Rickey didn't want anyone past thirty. Great as they once were, they were now past their prime. Rickey felt many of the young black players lacked the maturity to handle what would be a tough situation. Some were eliminated because the Dodger scouts felt they wouldn't be able to hit major league pitching.

By the spring of 1945 Rickey's search for a black player was in full swing. His scouts were going to Negro League games all over the country. Rickey eagerly awaited each report. After a while one name kept coming up. By that summer Jackie Robinson was being carefully considered by the shrewd Dodger general manager.

Actually Rickey wanted to know the names of five or six of the best black ballplayers. He was certain that once the "color line" was broken other teams would follow. He wanted to be able to sign up the top black players right away. But he needed to know the one outstanding player who would be able to pave the way for the rest.

Three of his scouts were particularly excited about Jackie. One said he was the best bunter he'd ever seen. Another said he was the best two-strike hitter in baseball — white or black. The only question was Jackie's throwing arm. One scout suggested he be switched to second base, where the throw to first was shorter. Rickey sent someone to watch every game Jackie played for a month, paying particular attention to his arm. The report came back that Jackie could play second base with any major league club. This was enough to convince Rickey to look into what kind of person Jackie Robinson was.

He was hoping to find a player with a college education. Jackie was qualified on that score. Rickey contacted friends in California who checked into Jackie's years in Pasadena and UCLA. Their reports said that Jackie had a reputation for being arrogant and cocky. Some said his "number one trouble was that he would argue with and talk back to white officials and players." But Rickey knew the only reason these characteristics were considered faults was because Robinson was black. ". . . he had done wrongly only because he was colored. If he had been white he would have been . . . spirited, [an] aggressive competitor. Because he was black his aggressiveness was considered offensive by some people . . . but not me. . . ." Rickey said.

Rickey wanted a mature person and the twenty-six-year-old Robinson was that. Rickey was also satisfied that he had the necessary drive and determination. It showed in everything he did, on and off the field. Rickey's investigation was thorough and he was satisfied he had his man.

Rickey sent Clyde Sukeforth, one of his top scouts, to watch Robinson play with the Monarchs. He wanted Sukeforth to convince Jackie to come back and meet with him. Rickey still had nagging worries about Jackie's arm and wanted Sukeforth to take a look at it, by watching Jackie go to the right and make the long throw to first. Sukeforth was sworn to absolute secrecy — but even he didn't know the truth. He thought the secrecy was about scouting players for Rickey's new Negro League.

It was late August when Sukeforth arrived in Chicago. The Kansas City Monarchs were playing the Chicago American Giants in Comiskey Park. At first Jackie didn't believe Sukeforth was a scout for the Dodgers. It was hard to believe that someone would come all the way from New York just to see him play. Unfortunately Jackie had injured his shoulder. Sukeforth couldn't see him throw, and Jackie wasn't even going to play that day.

Sukeforth tried to convice Jackie to come back with him to New York. He told Jackie that Branch Rickey wanted to meet with him tomorrow. At first Jackie didn't want to leave the team. Sukeforth argued that Jackie wasn't playing anyway because of his shoulder injury, so he wouldn't be hurting anyone by his absence. And the Dodgers would be taking care of all expenses. Finally Sukeforth convinced the suspicious Robinson to come back with him.

Jackie was worried about his salary. He was making $100 a week and he didn't want to risk losing it because of some wild-goose chase to Brooklyn.

Jackie Robinson and Branch Rickey met in Rickey's office the morning of August 28, 1945. The first thing the Dodgers' general manager wanted to know was if Jackie had a girlfriend. Jackie was surprised to be asked something so personal so quickly into their talk. After Jackie told Rickey that he was engaged, Rickey wanted to know all about Rachel. Then he switched topics. What kind of agreement did Jackie have with the Kansas City Monarchs? Did he have a contract? How did he get paid? Then Rickey told Jackie why he wanted to meet him.

It wasn't because of any new Negro League. ". . . I've sent for you because I'm interested in having you as a candidate for the Brooklyn National League club. I think you can play in the major leagues . . ." Jackie was surprised but not completely. He had suspected that the time was coming when something like this would happen.

A top Dodger scout coming to see him made him think something important was going on. Now he knew what it was.

Rickey said he wasn't worried about Jackie's baseball ability. He was concerned with the rest. He and Jackie would be fighting alone. The other owners would be against them and so would most of the players. Rickey wanted Jackie to understand how much courage would be required. He began pacing around the room, dramatizing the situations Jackie would find himself in . . . *You're up at the plate in a crucial situation. The first pitch is a high inside fastball that's comin' right for your head. The next thing you know you're eating dirt. What will you do? Or, you're playing second and a guy hits a line drive to right. He rounds first, stretching it into a double. The throw comes in and the play is close. The collision brings the crowd to its feet. The other player jumps up and starts screaming at you. Do you scream back? Hit him? What happens when you're playing shortstop and the guy on first takes off trying to steal second. He's coming in spike-first and he cuts your leg and you know he did it on purpose. Then, the guy gets up and looks at you and says, "How do you like that, nigger boy?"*

Rickey never stood still, pacing around the room, puffing his cigar, and sometimes coming so close their faces were only inches apart. Jackie had heard it all before and he knew what he'd *like* to do. He knew what he'd done in the past.

In the past he'd made it clear you didn't mess with Jackie Robinson.

Jackie was surprised by how much Rickey knew about his past. They talked about his years at UCLA. Rickey said he had heard about Jackie's reputation for having a short fuse — especially when it had anything to do with the color of his skin. He sympathized with Jackie and he told him that's why he was bringing it up. Because Jackie was black and stood up for himself, he developed a reputation as having a short temper. Rickey told Jackie that he understood that if Jackie were white the same critics would just smile and say he was competitive.

Rickey was worried about whether or not Jackie could walk away from the abuse that was sure to come his way. Rickey believed that fighting back would work against Jackie. It would be just what the people who didn't want baseball to be integrated hoped would happen. The first time Jackie went out to the mound because a pitcher threw right at him — the first time there was a scuffle on the base paths — the first time he was thrown out of a game over a call — it would all be over. His playing ability would get lost in the stories about the arguments, the flare-ups, and the fist fights. It wasn't working, people would say. Blacks and whites just don't belong together. Blacks just aren't mature enough. And the playing field wasn't the only place Rickey saw trouble.

Traveling in the white major leagues would probably be the worst part of it. Hotel clerks would tell Jackie he couldn't sleep there because he was black. And they'd be as rude about it as possible. When he'd been traveling by bus for hours in the darkest of night, all he'd be able to do sometimes was think about how hungry he was. Then he'd run into a restaurant manager telling him how he couldn't eat with the rest of the team. Maybe it would be better, the manager would explain, if Jackie came around back and ate in the kitchen with the help. Or maybe he could just stay on the bus and someone would bring him a sandwich.

They had been talking for almost three hours. Actually Rickey had been talking for almost three hours. Jackie had thought he understood as well as anyone how important it was that the first black major league baseball player succeed. Rickey had impressed him with the seriousness of the situation. He wanted to be as honest with Rickey as Rickey had been with him. He wasn't as nervous now as he had been at first. "Mr. Rickey, do you want a ballplayer who's afraid to fight back?" "No," Rickey said, "I want a ballplayer with guts enough *not* to fight back." Jackie would have to be willing to turn the other cheek. Any fighting back would have to be done with his bat and his glove, not with his fist and his mouth.

Jackie had begun to like and trust Rickey. He was impressed by his sincerity. Rickey was certain he had made the right choice: Jackie Robinson had the intelligence and personality to be the pioneer he was looking for. The only question was whether or not he was willing to do it. Jackie had always enjoyed challenges and now he was being offered the biggest one of his life. He looked at Rickey with a steady gaze and said in a calm voice: "Mr. Rickey, I think I can play ball in Montreal. I think I can play ball in Brooklyn. But you're a better judge of that than I am. If you want to take this gamble, I will promise you there will be no incident." It was a promise he never broke.

Rickey and Robinson agreed on a contract with the Montreal Royals, the top Dodger farm team. Jackie would get a $3,500 bonus for signing and $600 a month. If he made it in Montreal, his next step would be the big leagues.

This was the beginning of one of the longest and closest relationships in the history of sports. Over the years it would be described as father/son by some and teacher/student by others. It was a relationship built on continual and mutual respect.

Two months later, on October 23, 1945, the signing of Jackie Robinson was made public. The president of the Montreal Royals said that he had a "very important announcement that would affect baseball from coast to coast." The reporters gathered in his office that day were eager to hear the news.

The Royals' president, Hector Racine, introduced Jackie Robinson and said that they had signed him as shortstop for their club. "We made this step for two reasons. First, because we think of him . . . as a ballplayer. Second, we think it a point of fairness." For a moment the room was silent. Then, the reporters exploded from their seats and raced to phone in the story. When they returned they were allowed to ask Jackie questions.

Although Jackie appeared calm, he was nervous inside. He told them he felt like a guinea pig but was honored to have been chosen to play such an important role. He pointed out that he had spent most of his athletic days playing in integrated situations. Yes, he expected problems, but he was willing to confront them so he could do something for his race. The reporters were impressed. Their articles said that he seemed intelligent and confident without being arrogant.

FIGHT FOR ROBINSON MAY SPLIT BASE-BALL RIGHT OPEN, the *New York Post* declared. It was the most controversial sports story of the year. Newspaper and radio reporters scurried around trying to get reactions to the signing.

Branch Rickey and Jackie Robinson signing the historic contract that finally broke baseball's color barrier

Those reactions came fast and furiously. Some people suggested that white ballplayers would be driven from baseball because blacks would take over. Some said it just wouldn't work. There would be problems on the road when players had to live side by side.

Black players were also critical. Some felt there were players in the Negro Leagues who were better and more experienced than Jackie, who had played only one year of serious baseball.

Other people were critical of Rickey's choice, or so they said. They brought up Jackie's past with UCLA and the army, saying he was a troublemaker. Although few had actually seen him play, they agreed that he didn't have what it took. He was a 1000-to-1 chance. *The Sporting News* said that, at twenty-six, Robinson was too old for a rookie. They said he would soon find himself over his head in organized baseball.

The owners of the Negro League teams were also angry. It would ruin their businesses, they accurately predicted. They didn't want to hear any of this talk about how it was going to benefit their race. All they knew was that it wasn't going to benefit their pocketbooks. The Kansas City Monarchs said Rickey had no right to sign a player they had under contract. They hadn't even been given the courtesy of being notified. The major league white owners were also worried about the future of the Negro Leagues. If the Leagues folded, the money the major league owners made renting their ballparks to black teams would be lost. Rickey was killing baseball, they said. ("You run your club, and I'll run mine," was Rickey's reply.)

It was true that being deprived of that rental money would hurt the white owners financially. However, the real reason they protested so loudly was that they were, by and large, racists. Major league team owners believed that black people were inferior to white people. They didn't want to have anything to do with them on or off the baseball field.

The Dodgers were not surprised by the comments. Branch Rickey's son, nicknamed the "Twig" by sportswriters, issued a blunt statement. He said that the Dodgers had signed Jackie because they thought he could help them win. They weren't looking for trouble, but they were prepared to lose some of their Southern players who just didn't feel they could play with a black man. "Some players now with us may even quit, but they'll be back in baseball after they work a year or two in a cotton mill." Take it or leave it, the Twig was saying.

Not all white or all Southern players were hostile. Many said they wished Robinson luck and meant it. "Pee Wee" Reese, the Dodger shortstop, was from Kentucky. He heard the news while on a U.S. Navy ship returning from the Pacific. The fact that Jackie was black wasn't as important to Reese as the fact that he played shortstop. Those who hoped for a negative response from the popular Dodger were disappointed. When his ship docked, Reese met with reporters. With a smile he told them, "Just my luck, the first Negro to be signed to a contract in modern organized baseball not only has to be signed by the Brooklyn organization, but he also had to be a shortstop." In one sentence Reese had made it shortstop versus shortstop rather than white man versus black man.

Rickey emphasized that he had signed Jackie because he wanted to win a pennant, not because he wanted to integrate baseball. "When I go after baseball players . . . I never notice the color of [their] skins. I never meant to be a crusader. . . . My purpose is to be fair. . . . My objective is to win games." This, of course, wasn't entirely true. Rickey *was* a crusader, campaigning against things he believed were wrong, whether it won him games or not. Winning was part of it but not the heart of it.

In general the decision was a popular one. Many fans felt it was about time America truly became the land of liberty and equality.

Jackie's family was proud, but they were frightened because they realized what Jackie would have to go through.

Wendell Smith, one of the great black sportswriters of the day, said: "Jackie has the hopes . . . and ambitions of thirteen million black Americans heaped upon his broad and sturdy shoulders."

7
The Minors

In February, 1946, Jackie and Rachel were married at a large church wedding in Los Angeles. Soon after, they headed for Daytona Beach, the Dodgers' training camp.

Rachel was nervous about traveling in the South. She had heard of the things that happened to blacks who didn't watch their step — and even to those who did. Thirty blacks had been lynched that year by white mobs who wouldn't bother to wait for a trial.

Their flight was almost as bad as Rachel had feared it would be. No one would serve them food in New Orleans, where they had to wait for a connecting flight. The run-down "colored" hotel they finally found was so dirty that neither of them could get any sleep. In Pensacola, Florida, they were taken off the plane so two white people could have their seats. Arguing did them little good. They took a bus to Jacksonville, Florida. They had to sit in the back because the front was reserved for "whites only." The seats in the back were different from the ones up front. They were more uncomfortable and didn't recline. The ride to Jacksonville took sixteen hours. The Robinsons were hungry and tired most of the trip. When they finally arrived, Jackie was three days late.

The baseball season began in Florida, where white teams had their training camps. Like most Southern states in the 1940s, Florida was segregated. Whites were kept separate from blacks, especially when it came to traveling accommodations. Hotels, restaurants, and waiting rooms either didn't allow blacks or had an area assigned to them. Blacks could watch whites play baseball, but only from separate sections. And they could only watch whites play whites and blacks play blacks. Competition between the races on the playing fields was strictly forbidden — not only by custom, but by law. Rickey was aware of this, but he couldn't do anything about where spring training began. He did as much groundwork as possible over the winter, talking with local officials to make Jackie's arrival as smooth as possible.

The Florida newspapers made it clear that

Blacks and whites were kept segregated in the South by Jim Crow laws.

Jackie was not welcomed. They liked their seg-regated Southern ways, and now here *he* was to change all that. Hotel and restaurant owners said they weren't going to treat Jackie Robinson dif-ferently from any other black.

The Royals' first game in Jacksonville was can-celled. The head of the playground and recreation committee said that whites and blacks could not compete against each other on city-owned play-grounds. In another game the chief of police walked right on the field and informed the Mon-treal manager that Robinson had to be removed. To keep the peace he was.

Rickey didn't want to become involved with legal issues in Florida — not if he could avoid it. "I'm going there to play ball, not to live," he said. He did whatever he could to avoid problems. He had Jackie and Rachel stay at the home of a black political leader. But Rickey knew they would have to make a stand somewhere. The president of the Montreal Royals issued a statement: "It will be all or nothing with the Montreal club. Jackie Robinson go[es] with the team, or there's no game." Rickey knew that Florida politicians were beginning to feel the heat put on them by Northern newspapers who were critical of what was going on. He also knew that he had econom-ics on his side. Daytona city officials had acted better than most in making Jackie and the Royals feel welcome. Having the Dodgers spend spring training there every year brought a lot of money into the community. The officials were worried that the Dodgers might go somewhere else.

Jackie had so many things to worry about, he wasn't sure where to begin. While the tension swirled all around him, he struggled to concentrate on baseball. He still had to make the team. His first day at spring training reminded him of how he had felt his first day of school — nervous and unsure of himself. There were over 200 white ballplayers on the field, all trying out for a position. As far as baseball playing was concerned, Jackie was just one of the guys. When reporters asked him if he was after the Dodger shortstop position, Pee Wee Reese's job, he told them he was worried about making the *Montreal* club, not Brooklyn. He wanted to do well so badly that he tried too hard and developed a sore arm. He had to be switched to second, but his arm was too sore to make the throw from there, too. They moved him to first base. Now, on top of everything else, he was making his debut in spring training at a position he had never played before.

The exhibition season ended without any proof of Jackie's ability. He was plagued by a sore arm and his hitting was erratic. There was still plenty of doubts about his ability to play in the big leagues.

April 18, 1946, Jersey City, New Jersey. Jackie Robinson was about to play his first game in organized baseball. Thirty-five thousand fans jammed Roosevelt Stadium to watch the Royals play the Jersey City Giants. Newspaper reporters were out in full force. Jackie grounded out his first trip to the plate. But in the top of the third, with men on first and second, he hit the first pitch for a 340-foot three-run home run. In the fifth inning he bunted, stole second, and went to third on an infield out. With Rickey's instructions to be daring on the base paths buzzing in his ears, Jackie pranced off third base. When the pitcher began his windup he streaked for home, pulled up and ran back, sliding into third just in time. On his third pitch, the pitcher balked and Jackie scored. He singled his last time up and went to third when the ball glanced off the second baseman's glove. Again he was balked home, bringing the crowd to its feet. Jackie Robinson's reputation as the most daring base runner in baseball history was beginning.

Jackie and Rachel had grown closer during this tense period. Their difficulties showed them that they were both fighters. Now that they were settled in Montreal they were able to relax a little. Rickey had not chosen Montreal by accident. Besides being the top Dodger farm team, Montreal was a city where Jackie and Rachel were likely to encounter the least amount of prejudice. Rachel was pregnant and they wanted to find a nice apartment. They were lucky enough to get a clean, sunny place in the French-Canadian section of the city. The people there had never seen a black person. They were curious but courteous and friendly. The Robinsons loved living in Montreal.

The Montreal Royals were a very good team even before Jackie joined. But he provided the fiery edge they needed and they coasted to the top of their division. The regular season had begun badly for Jackie in Baltimore, the southernmost city the Royals traveled to. Other than ugly incidents in Syracuse, things cooled down once the season got under way.

A million fans came out in 1946 to watch the Royals play — a new minor league record.

By the end of the season the pressure had taken its toll. Jackie was worn out. He had trouble sleeping and Rachel was worried. For a while he actually thought about quitting. The strain of not striking back was getting to him. He talked it over with his family and his wife and decided to stick it out. A doctor he visited ordered ten days' bed rest. With the Royals already on their way to the playoffs, the timing seemed ideal. But Jackie was leading the league in batting and he was afraid that if he stayed home people would say he was afraid of losing his batting title in the last days. He played.

Jackie's .349 average led the league. He had 66 RBIs and scored 113 runs, tied for the top spot.

While playing for the minor league Montreal Royals, Jackie
Robinson led the league in batting.

His .985 fielding percentage at second also led the league. He was second in stolen bases and had made bunting into an art form.

The Royals were going to play the Louisville Colonels in the Little World Series, as it was called. The Series would begin in Louisville, Kentucky. Once again Jackie Robinson was heading south to play baseball.

The Louisville club owners limited the number of blacks who could attend each game. They said they were afraid of racial conflict. Jackie was booed and hounded by the Louisville fans. He played badly.

The first three games in Louisville were difficult for Jackie. The more the fans got on him with their shouts of "nigger," the worse he played. The Royals lost two of the first three games and headed back to Montreal. Their fans welcomed them back with open arms. They had followed the stories in the papers each day about how Jackie was being treated and had come to show their support.

The Royals won the next three games and the Series. Jackie scored the winning run in the seventh game. It took more than an hour for him to fight his way through the sea of fans who rejoiced at his playing and the team's victory.

Jackie Robinson had shown that a black man could play organized baseball and the world wouldn't come to an end.

8
Rookie of the Year and MVP

On April 10, 1947, the Dodgers and the Royals were playing an exhibition game at Ebbets Field. A press release was handed out during the game: "Brooklyn announces the purchase of the contract of Jack Roosevelt Robinson from Montreal." Jackie would be getting $5,000 his first year.

Jackie's year with the Royals had been a success. He showed that he was not only an outstanding baseball player but a person of integrity. Clay Hooper, Jackie's Mississippi-born manager at Montreal, had been very unhappy when he was forced to accept Jackie at the beginning of the year. But by the end of the season he had gone to Jackie and told him, "You're a great ballplayer and a fine gentleman. You're the greatest com-

Jackie Robinson proudly wearing the uniform of the Brooklyn Dodgers

petitor I ever saw. It's been wonderful having you on the team." And Hooper meant every word.

Branch Rickey had done everything he could to make the move to the big leagues as smooth as possible for Jackie. The Royals and Dodgers played seven exhibition games that preseason. Rickey let Jackie know just how important he thought those games were. He wanted Jackie to go all out, hoping that the Dodgers would see just how good Robinson was. In the seven games he batted .625 and stole seven bases.

Rickey also worked behind the scenes. He met with Brooklyn's black leaders and told them that he was concerned about the reaction of the black community. He feared that black fans would be overenthusiastic. Rickey didn't want welcoming committees, parades, big signs, or anything else that would make Jackie's situation any more noticeable than it already was. Rickey also worried that black fans filling the ballparks and celebrating their new hero might cause white fans to stay away. Although some black leaders were insulted by what Rickey was saying, most agreed and a committee was formed. A slogan was adopted: "Don't spoil Jackie's chances."

The Robinsons were now a family of three. Jackie, Jr., had been born in November, 1947. Jackie and Rachel had enjoyed where they lived in Montreal but finding something nice in New York was a problem. They had to settle for a small

On opening day, Jackie received congratulations from many supporters, but he also received threats.

and dreary one-room apartment. Baby diapers hung in the bathroom, and when guests arrived toys were pushed under the furniture.

Five days after the announcement, number 42 took the field for the opening game of the season. There were 26,623 in attendance — over half were blacks waiting to see one of the most exciting events of their lifetime.

Jackie was tense and overeager. He was more concerned with his new position, first base, than he was with anything else. He was not happy playing first. Learning to play a new position at the same time he was trying to break into the big leagues was a nearly impossible task. But Rickey had no other choice. Eddie Stanky, the starting second baseman, was not only one of the best in the league, but a popular Dodger. Rickey wanted to avoid any talk about how blacks would take jobs away from white players. Also, by having Jackie play first base, Rickey felt opposing players would be less able to spike him. Certainly less than if he were playing second. Jackie would just have to learn on the job. He went 0 for 3 his first game, continued to press too hard, and started the season with an 0 for 20 batting slump.

Off the field Jackie kept to himself, dressing in the corner of the locker room. He didn't talk to anyone unless they talked to him. He decided it would be best that way, especially at first. He didn't want to walk around hoping people would be friendly to him. He had too much pride for that.

On the road he usually ate alone in his hotel room. He stayed behind when the rest of the players headed for the movies or the hotel bar. He didn't join in the card games, even though he loved to play. Traveling on the train to an away game he ate by himself or with one of the black reporters who traveled with the team. It was a lonely life.

One of the first players to be friendly to Jackie was Pee Wee Reese. As soon as it was announced that Jackie was going to play for the Dodgers, Pee Wee heard from his friends back home in Louisville, Kentucky. They told him it just wasn't right for a "good Southern boy" to be playing ball next to a black player. Pee Wee thought long and hard about the situation. He decided that his friends were wrong and that there was "room enough in baseball for both of us." Later, after he got to know Jackie, he felt even more strongly about it.

Some Dodger players were so upset about having to play with a black man that they circulated a secret petition. The petition declared that those who signed it would not play on the same team with a black player. Five or six players signed the petition but it didn't go any further. Reese refused to sign and so did Duke Snider. Snider was from Southern California and Jackie, he explained, was one of his heroes.

Jackie's relationship with his teammates changed about the same time that his playing did. At first he had played cautiously, which wasn't his style. On June 24th he stole home for the first time. By then he was already hitting pretty well. He was batting .315 and was becoming one of the most feared base runners in the league. The other Dodgers were impressed by his will to win. Like other truly great athletes in the history of team sports, he made the players around him play better. The usually serious Jackie began to relax a little. He even started to joke around after games. His teammates invited him to join them in card games and he accepted. His fellow Dodgers soon found out he was as competitive at the card table as he was on the baseball diamond.

Although the atmosphere in the Dodger clubhouse improved, there was no letup with the competition. Early in the season the owner of the Phillies called Rickey and warned him that there would be trouble. He suggested it would be best if Robinson were kept on the bench. Rickey had no intention of keeping Robinson on the bench. During the three-game series the Phillies insulted Jackie constantly and called him names: nigger, coon, darkie. They shouted from the dugout, asking him why he wasn't home cleaning out bathrooms or picking cotton. The worst culprit of all was the Philadelphia manager, who was from Alabama.

By the second game of the series some of the Dodgers had listened to about enough. Ed Stanky started shouting back to the Phillies bench: Why didn't they pick on someone who could fight back? Jackie's hands were tied, and Stanky wanted them to know he thought they were yellow. Jackie had to fight the burning desire to stride across the field and take on half the team.

The incidents with the Phillies were widely covered in the newspapers. A photo session was set up so that Chapman, the Phillies manager, and Jackie would be seen shaking hands. Jackie swallowed his pride because Mr. Rickey asked him to. Rickey said it would be in the best interests of baseball to get the incident behind them. Both men agreed to have their photographs taken. Some stories say that Jackie refused to shake hands with Chapman. Some say that Chapman refused to shake hands with Jackie. Some actually say that they were photographed shaking hands, but there is no such photograph. There is only a photograph of two men not looking at each other, posing for a publicity photo.

The Philadelphia incident drew the Dodgers closer to one another. It marked a turning point in their attitudes toward Jackie. They sympathized with what he was going through and the restraint he showed in not striking back. They began to respect him.

In May the Dodgers were scheduled to play the

St. Louis Cardinals. The Cardinals threatened to strike if Robinson was in the lineup. Ford Frick, president of the National League, took an immediate and strong stand: "If you do this," he told the striking players, "you will be suspended from the league. You will find that the friends that you think you have in the press box will not support you, that you will be outcasts. I do not care if half the league strikes." There was no strike.

Throughout that first year things were difficult for Jackie Robinson off the field as well as on. There were crank phone calls and letters threatening Rachel and Jackie, Jr., with violence and kidnapping. Jackie and Rachel talked frequently while he was on the road. Jackie just didn't know if he could take it anymore. He showed little emotion to those around him, but inside he was like a volcano ready to erupt.

The abuse he took on the field was subtle. A hard tag on the side of the head while sliding into a base. Pitches aimed right for his head in an unimportant game with no one on base. Insults whispered behind a held-up glove.

But no matter how bad things got, Jackie and Rachel had decided it was worth it. The things he was accomplishing were too important. Jackie was being called the biggest gate attraction since Babe Ruth. Several attendance records were set that year. The first Saturday the Dodgers played the New York Giants at the Polo Grounds 52,000 turned out. It was the largest Saturday afternoon crowd in National League history. The Dodgers drew 1.8 million fans at home, setting a National League record. (It was the first of ten straight million-plus attendance years for the Dodgers.) Four other National League teams had record-breaking home attendance figures: New York, Boston, Pittsburgh, and St. Louis. Attendance figures for the league as a whole were up 3.4 million from the year before — which had been a banner year. It was all because of Jackie Robinson.

Blacks were coming to the games like they never had before, while white attendance figures were also up. As one writer put it, "Jackie's nimble, Jackie's quick, Jackie's making the turnstile click." Black fans, some who had never seen baseball before Jackie Robinson, cheered wildly if he hit a foul ball. A pop-up sometimes got a standing ovation. Some fans wore "I'm for Jackie" buttons. Wherever Jackie played it was an event for black families for miles around. They would travel as far as they had to to see him play. Before the year was out there were other blacks signed up for the big leagues. (In July Larry Doby became the first black player in the American League.)

That year the Dodgers won their first pennant since 1941. (Before the American and National League split into East and West divisions, winning the league championship was called "winning the pennant.")

Jackie finished the year with a .297 batting average and led the league in stolen bases. He was second in runs scored and his 12 home runs led the team. He showed the white major leagues how to bunt. He had 28 successful bunts, 14 for base hits. He appeared in 151 out of 154 games, more than anyone else on the team.

In October the Dodgers met the Yankees in what is considered one of the greatest World Series in history. There was a near no-hitter in the fourth game and in the sixth one of the most memorable catches ever — Al Gionfriddo's catch of Joe DiMaggio's line drive. Five of the seven games were close. The Yankees won the series in seven games.

The Sporting News, which had said earlier that Jackie would find himself over his head in the major leagues, named him Rookie of the Year.

During the off-season Jackie accepted speaking engagements around the country. Initially Rickey wouldn't let him do anything but play baseball. Hundreds of offers to endorse products or make commercials had to be turned down. Rickey didn't want people to be able to criticize Jackie for exploiting the situation. But by the end of the season Rickey let up on this rule. Jackie was glad because now that he was a father he could use the extra money.

Unfortunately Jackie ate more than his share of the roast beef, mashed potatoes with gravy, and rolls that were served at these banquets.

The next year, 1948, Jackie reported to spring training hopelessly out of shape. His weight had ballooned up to 220, 30 pounds overweight. He was fat and slow. He couldn't run and that affected his whole game.

He played himself back into shape by midseason, but the Dodgers ended up in third place. He still managed to hit .296 with 85 RBIs, 12 homers, and 22 stolen bases, and led the league with a .983 fielding average at second base. (Rickey had decided to trade Stanky.)

The next year Jackie reported to spring training in excellent shape. He was ready to play the best baseball of his life.

Jackie was shifted from batting second to fourth, cleanup. Jackie was a classic number-two hitter: He didn't strike out, could get down the line fast, and was a great bunter. Batting second the year before he had knocked in 85 RBIs — a lot for the number-two man in the order. But the Dodger management suspected that it was a waste having a clutch hitter bat so early in the lineup. What would happen if Jackie batted when there were more men on base? Putting Jackie in the cleanup spot turned out to be a brilliant move.

He tore up the league. His .342 average captured the batting title. He hammered 16 home runs, had 203 hits and 124 RBIs, and played in all 156 games.

Jackie was the most dangerous when he got on base. His 37 stolen bases led the league. He could go from first to third on a sacrifice and could score from first on a single. He made stealing home part of the game. He had a whole philosophy about it: Never plan it; don't do it unless there are two outs, the run is absolutely necessary, the pitcher is showing no signs of losing his stuff, and only do it when a right-handed batter is at the plate.

Jackie Robinson was not only a naturally gifted athlete, he was a student of the game. Opposing players had learned that Jackie would not be intimidated, and they stopped a lot of the cheap stuff that had been going on. He was now one of the best players in the game. His two million votes was tops on the 1949 All-Star team. He was named the Most Valuable Player in the National League.

Jackie could play all the infield positions

Jackie practicing his swing

Jackie in a rundown against the Cubs

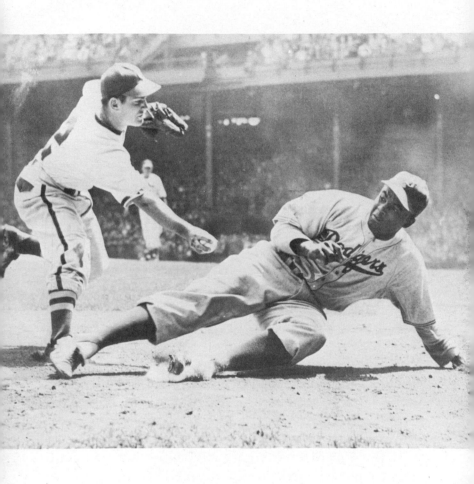

Safe!

9
The Real Jackie

In the summer of 1949 Jackie was asked to appear before the House Un-American Activities Committee. Since the end of World War II the United States and the Soviet Union had grown suspicious of each other. The U.S. government considered the Communist government of the U.S.S.R. to be hostile and aggressive. They would, it was felt, do anything to overthrow the American government and take over. This fear was shared by many people throughout the United States.

The Committee investigated what it considered un-American, pro-Soviet activities. Any American whom they felt suspicious of could be asked to appear at a hearing. These hearings were highly controversial because some Americans felt that what the Committee was doing was a violation of fundamental rights, which were protected by the Constitution.

Jackie had been asked to appear not to defend himself but to state his disagreement with Paul Robeson. Robeson was a well-known black actor who had recently said that black Americans should not fight in a war against Russia. He said this because he felt that blacks were not treated well in the United States. Robeson had visited the Soviet Union and come to believe that the Communist system of government was one that promised equality for all.

Being asked to testify against Robeson presented Jackie with a terrible dilemma. Jackie knew that he was being asked to represent those black Americans who didn't feel the way Robeson did. But he also knew that many *did* feel that way. They were tired of their second-class status. Jackie didn't want to be used by the Committee to help divide and conquer blacks. But he couldn't escape his belief that America was his country — faults and all.

On July 18, 1949, Jackie appeared before the Committee. He had carefully prepared his statement. Rachel sat behind him as he read it. He spoke about the progress that had been made and the long road yet to be traveled. He spoke of black

Americans and their feelings about segregation and discrimination. He could not agree with Robeson's statement, however:

> *I have too much invested in our country's welfare. . . . I cherish America. . . . but that doesn't mean we're going to stop fighting race discrimination in this country. . . . We can win our fight without the Communists and we don't need their help.*

The newspaper headlines told the story: *JACKIE ROBINSON, AMERICAN: JACKIE HITS ANOTHER HOME RUN.*

The articles didn't talk about how critical Jackie was of the racial situation in the United States. They only spoke about his disagreement with Robeson. Jackie's appearance was applauded by most, but he never felt certain he had done the right thing. A few years later he said that he "had grown wiser and closer to the painful truth about America's destructiveness . . . I have increased respect for Paul Robeson. . . . I believe he was sincerely trying to help his people."

For two years Jackie Robinson had taken all the abuse that was aimed his way. He was thrown at, spiked, spit on, and insulted by players, shouted at, booed, and threatened by fans. He decided enough was enough — he had paid his dues, and Branch Rickey agreed. Rickey told Jackie that he was free to say and do as he pleased. He had proved what he had to prove. Jackie told his teammates: ". . . I'm here to play baseball and from this point on I take nothing else."

Jackie had been feisty ever since he was little. During the past two years he had been forced to behave like someone else. Although he had known how difficult the situation would be and had no regrets, that didn't make him like it any better. From now on he wasn't going to take it — he was going to give some of it back.

People were surprised to see what Jackie was *really* like. He had appeared to be quiet, almost shy. Now he was outspoken, almost blunt. He spoke out on any issue that concerned him.

During spring training in 1949 Jackie stood toe-to-toe with a rookie pitcher he felt had thrown at him. Two days later a New York newspaper article said, "This is no longer the meek, inoffensive, uncomplaining Robinson who first appeared in the big league."

By 1951 Jackie was considered one of the most controversial players in the game. Jackie was always opinionated and he began to criticize sportswriters. He called them "careless" and accused them of distorting the truth.

Jackie had changed and the situation was becoming heated. Baseball Commissioner Chandler spoke with Jackie, cautioning him to behave as he had his first year. This conversation became a controversy. Some sportswriters spoke out. Did Jackie have to behave himself because he was black? Maybe he was aggressive and fiesty, but so were a lot of white players. Was the commissioner going to talk to them? But many in baseball started to think of Jackie as a troublemaker.

Jackie helped black kids at New York City's Harlem YMCA improve their recreation program. His weekly sports program reached thousands more. In 1950 *The Jackie Robinson Story*, in which he played himself, had its movie premiere in New York.

In 1953 Jackie appeared on a program called *Youth Wants to Know*. He was asked about the fact that there were still no blacks playing for the New York Yankees. At the time there were seven major league teams and a total of twenty-three black players. As always his answer left the listener with no doubt where he stood: "I have always felt ... that the Yankees ... have been giving Negroes the runaround."

Jackie was no longer the only black on the Dodger team. He began to talk to his black teammates about what he felt were their obligations. Not all of them saw it the way Jackie wanted

A Dodger in Hollywood: Jackie on the set of *The Jackie Robinson Story*.

them to see it. Some resented him, feeling that no one had appointed him their leader.

But the close relationship that had developed between Jackie and his teammates remained strong. The difficulties they had gone through those first few years created a lasting bond. The Dodgers of the 1950s were considered a special team in baseball history. Jackie agreed: "It sometimes struck me that Mr. Rickey must have gone out and rounded up the ideal teammates for me. I know I couldn't have picked better guys to break in with."

Before a game with the Cincinnati Reds, Jackie received a letter threatening his life. The writer warned that if Jackie took the field for the game he would be shot. The Dodger manager read the letter aloud to all the players because he wanted them to know the horrible pressure Jackie had to endure. Gene Hermanski thought about the situation and had an idea: "Why don't we all go out on the field wearing number 42 [Jackie's number] on our uniforms and then the person won't know which one of us to shoot?"

On the field, however, things *had* changed. Opposing players realized that Jackie was not going to be intimidated. They were forced to concentrate on beating him at the game.

Jackie continued to play aggressive baseball. He wanted to win every game without exception. In one game the Dodgers had an eleven-run lead

The Dodger infield. From left: Spider Jorgensen, Eddie Stanky,
Pee Wee Reese, and Jackie

and the Dodgers' pitcher let up and walked the bases loaded. Jackie came over to the mound and told the pitcher: "If you don't want to pitch, go back to the hotel."

Jackie's desire to win was also illustrated by his behavior in the 1951 play-offs with the Giants.

The Dodgers had a lengthy lead toward the end of the season. Everyone thought they were a cinch to win the pennant. Miraculously the Giants tied them during the last game of the year and forced a three-game play-off to decide the pennant winner.

The Giants won the first game and the Dodgers the second. Game three became one of the most dramatic games in the history of baseball.

The Dodgers were leading 4–1 going into the bottom of the ninth. The first two men up singled. With one out there was a double to left center making the score 4–2. With men on second and third Bobby Thompson was up with Willie Mays on deck. The Dodgers changed pitchers, bringing in Ralph Branca. Thompson hit Branca's second pitch for a game-winning, pennant-clinching home run. Throughout Brooklyn, fans who had been glued to their radios were stunned. The fans in the stands erupted as the Giants celebrated and the Dodgers made their way to the safety of their dugout. One Dodger remained at his position. Jackie Robinson, hands on his hips, was watching Thompson circle the bases making sure he touched every base. Only then did he walk off the field admitting defeat.

The next year the Dodgers won the pennant by four and a half games. The year after, 1953, they won by thirteen games.

The 1955 Dodgers were considered one of the best baseball teams ever. There were All-Stars at eight positions. Gil Hodges, the first baseman, hit .302, had 122 RBIs, and 31 home runs. Junior Gilliam, the young black lead-off man, had scored 125 runs. Pee Wee Reese batted .271 and stole 22 bases. Billy Cox, at third, batted .291. Jackie hit .329 and had 95 RBIs. Duke Snider, the star center fielder, had 42 home runs and hit .336 while driving in 126 runs. Carl Furillo, called the "Rifle" because of his fine throwing arm, patrolled right field while hitting .344 and knocking in 92 runs. Roy Campanella, the Dodgers' black catcher, hit .312, had 41 home runs, 142 RBIs, and was voted the Most Valuable Player in the National League. They clinched the pennant on September 13th, earlier than any National League team ever had.

Nineteen fifty-five marked the first time the Dodgers won the World Series, beating their hated crosstown rivals, the Yankees, in seven games.

By 1955, however, Jackie was often left out of the starting lineup. He didn't play in a third of the games. Part of the reason was his open dislike of Walter Alston, now the Dodgers' manager. Alston was not a very emotional manager and the newspapers reported Jackie's comment that he was a "wooden Indian." Jackie had a series of injuries that slowed him down. Thirty-six and now in his ninth season, he was beginning to lose some of his confidence. He thought seriously about retiring.

Nineteen fifty-six wasn't much better. Jackie was used as a utility player at third, second, first, and in the outfield. He batted .275. His base-running savvy and aggressiveness still figured in key games, but it wasn't enough.

Branch Rickey resigned in the fall of 1950 after losing a power struggle for control of the team. Walter O'Malley, a tough New York lawyer, took over. As soon as Rickey left, Jackie's troubles with the Dodger management began. O'Malley and Rickey hadn't liked each other, and O'Malley didn't want anything to do with "Rickey's people." It was unpopular to speak nicely about Branch Rickey, but Jackie Robinson wasn't about to start doing the popular thing now.

By 1956 there were two rumors circulating that concerned loyal Brooklyn fans. One was the incredible idea that the Dodgers were thinking of moving out of Brooklyn — to Los Angeles. The other was that Jackie Robinson was going to retire.

Soon after, all of Brooklyn and most of the baseball world was shocked to learn that the Dodgers had *traded* Jackie Robinson! If that wasn't bad enough, they had traded him to the New York Giants. The Giants gave the Dodgers $35,000 and a little-known pitcher named Dick Littlefield.

In January, 1957, Jackie announced his retirement from baseball. He had considered going to the Giants, but in an article in *Look* magazine he explained: "My legs are gone and I know it. . . . [the Giants] ballclub needs . . . rebuilding. It needs youth. It doesn't need me. It would be unfair to the Giant owners to take their money."

After the trade Jackie visited his family in Pasadena. He had always kept in touch, visiting whenever he could and calling frequently. They were proud of him and followed the newspaper stories and the radio broadcasts about him as often as possible. Mack was proud of the way his brother never forgot the family.

Jackie Robinson played in the major leagues for only ten years. When he began playing for the Dodgers he was twenty-eight — old for a rookie. He knew he had to be good right away, and he maintained an almost constant level of intensity.

The Dodgers won the pennant six of the ten years Jackie was with them. They never finished below third.

Jackie Robinson batted over .300 six times, stole home twenty times, and scored over 100 runs six times. He was one of the best clutch hitters of all time and could hit for average or pull the ball with power. He stole bases and was always a threat to take the extra base. His daring base running changed the way baseball was played in the National League. He rattled pitchers and kept constant pressure on the opposing team.

Hall of Famer Ralph Kiner described Jackie Robinson the baseball player better than anyone else: "[He] was the only player I ever saw who could completely turn a game around by himself."

Jackie Robinson had played his last baseball game.

10
The Final Chapter

Jackie had been thinking about his retirement before receiving the phone call notifying him about the trade.

Look magazine had paid him $50,000 for the exclusive rights to the story of his retirement. Jackie had been secretly working on the article just days before the trade.

He had also finalized his agreement to work for Chock full o'Nuts. Chock full o'Nuts was a New York City-based chain of coffee shops that specialized in excellent coffee, clean surroundings, and service with a smile. By the time the trade was announced, Jackie had decided to retire from the world of baseball and enter the world of business.

Jackie and some of his young fans

Jackie was now Vice President, Director of Personnel, at a salary of $40,000 a year. He had changed uniforms — this one consisted of a white shirt, suit, and a tie.

The job was just what Jackie was looking for. He wanted a job where he could do something and not just be a famous name. There was plenty to do at Chock full o' Nuts. Jackie spent time traveling from store to store, talking with the employees, seventy percent of whom were black. After a while he got to know what their problems were. If there was something he could do to help he would. One of his projects was a summer camp for the children of the employees. The people who worked at Chock full o' Nuts could see that Jackie came from a background similiar to theirs and understood their problems.

Now, at last, Jackie could spend more time with his family. While he was playing, baseball was his first priority. When he wasn't at Ebbets Field, the Dodgers' ballpark, he always seemed to be on a train traveling to or returning from an away game. His first daughter, Sharon, had been born in January, 1950. Two years later, in May, David was born. Fortunately, as the family had grown, Jackie had earned enough money to afford more space. In his second year with the Dodgers, 1948, the family lived in a sunny duplex apartment in Brooklyn. Later they were able to save enough money to buy their first house in St. Al-

Jackie Robinson reading to his family. From left: Jackie; Jackie, Jr.; Sharon; David; and Rachel Robinson.

bans, Long Island where they lived for five years. When Jackie retired from baseball, Rachel decided to return to college and earn her master's degree in psychological nursing. They bought a new house in North Stamford, Connecticut, which had twelve rooms and stood on five acres.

Jackie was considered a spokesman for black Americans. The civil rights movement was growing, and he was often asked his views on the momentous events of the day. Many of the black leaders had grown up hearing and reading about Jackie's success against terrific odds. These same people were now part of a national movement to gain the rights they believed were guaranteed them by the Constitution of the United States.

Jackie attacked the state of racial relations in the world he had just left. He pointed out that all major league teams still weren't integrated. (A year later, in 1959, the Boston Red Sox would become the last team to sign a black player.) He criticized the slow progress of school integration. In 1954 the United States Supreme Court had ruled in the case of *Brown* v. *the Board of Education*. The Court had decided that schools that kept blacks and whites separated resulted in unequal education and were therefore unconstitutional. It was a critical turning point in American history. Schools, the Court was saying, have to be integrated. But Southern states were slow to obey the law of the land.

*   *   *

Jackie also did a weekly radio show and wrote a column three times a week for the *New York Post*. The controversial column had a wide readership and Jackie received many letters each week. He wrote about politics, baseball, international affairs, and the upcoming Presidential race between Senator John F. Kennedy and Vice President Richard Nixon.

Both candidates wanted Jackie's support. His backing meant a lot of votes in a race that was sure to be close. Never one to do what was expected of him, Jackie chose to support Richard Nixon, the Republican candidate. It was a move that took many people by surprise. Rachel, Jackie's wife, supported Kennedy. Jackie had met with both men before he had decided. He said that Nixon had the better civil rights voting record. Kennedy, he said, "couldn't or wouldn't look me straight in the eye."

He left Chock full o' Nuts to devote full time to the Nixon campaign.

Asked if he missed baseball, he said not at all. He said he never watched a game either on TV or in person.

Throughout the campaign Nixon had little to say about the racial situation. Some people felt he had decided not to support the civil rights movement, fearing that if he did he would lose more white votes than he would gain black votes.

110

When Nixon lost, Jackie was out of a job. Governor Nelson Rockefeller, who had met Jackie when he was with Chock full o'Nuts, offered him a position with the New York State Athletic Commission. Later Jackie also worked with the Rockefeller Foundation.

Jackie continued to be involved in the civil rights movement. Years before the sit-ins that marked the beginning of the movement, Jackie had staged his own sit-in. Asked to leave the "whites only" waiting room in the Greensboro, North Carolina, airport, he had refused. The Greensboro authorities backed down and Jackie was allowed to wait where he wanted until he boarded his plane.

Dr. Martin Luther King's Southern Christian Leadership Conference (SCLC) was one of the groups helping to organize the movement. On March 29, 1960, they ran a full-page ad in *The New York Times*. It was hoped that the ad would give moral support to black students in Alabama who were protesting the racial situation there. Jackie made sure his name was added to the list of celebrities and political leaders who had signed the ad in support of the cause.

By the early sixties, the nature of the civil rights movement had changed. Tired of begging for their rights, many blacks, especially the young ones, were demanding them. Because of his sup-

Jackie and Vice-President Hubert Humphrey during the 1968 election campaign

port of Nixon, Rockefeller, and the Republican Party, Jackie was considered a conservative at a time when most blacks were liberal Democrats. Once again Jackie was in the minority.

Jackie traveled across the country speaking on behalf of the National Association for the Advancement of Colored People (NAACP) and the National Conference of Christians and Jews. He addressed college groups and worked with Dr. Martin Luther King, Jr., although he didn't always agree with him.

In the summer of 1962 Jackie Robinson was inducted into Baseball's Hall of Fame, in his first year of eligibility. His plaque reads:

JACK ROOSEVELT ROBINSON
Brooklyn, N.L. 1947–1956
Leading N.L. batter in 1949. Holds fielding mark for second baseman play in 150 or more games with .992. Led N.L. in stolen bases in 1947 and 1949. Most Valuable Player in 1949. Lifetime batting average .311. Joint record holder for most double plays by second baseman, 137 in 1951. Led second basemen in double plays 1949–50–51–52.

During the ceremony Jackie asked three people to stand with him: his mother, Mallie Robinson, Rachel, and Branch Rickey.

Three years later Branch Rickey died. One of the things written on his Hall of Fame plaque is: *Brought Jackie Robinson to Brooklyn in 1947.* "Surely," he had said, "God was with me when I picked Jackie. . . . He really did understand the responsibility he carried . . . he had the intelligence of knowing how to handle himself under adversity. Above all he had what the boys call guts, real guts."

In 1971 the Robinson's twenty-four-year-old son Jackie, Jr., was killed in a single-car accident. The family was stunned and the tragedy worsened Jackie's already failing health.

A year later Jackie attended the funeral of his friend and former teammate, Dodger first baseman Gil Hodges. His appearance shocked those who hadn't seen him for a while. The diabetes he had struggled with all his life had caused him to deteriorate rapidly. He looked old — older than his years. His hair had been gray for quite a while and even walking seemed to be an effort. He had put on weight. His eyesight was so bad he could no longer drive.

Jackie threw out the first ball in the second game of the 1972 World Series. He appeared to be in pain. A fan asked him to sign his baseball. "I'm sorry," Jackie said, "I can't see it. I'd be sure if I wrote only to mess up the other names you have on it." The fan pushed the ball back. "There

Bowie Kuhn watches as Jackie throws the ball out at the second game of the 1972 World Series.

are no other names, Mr. Robinson. The only one I want is yours."

Nine days later, on October 24, 1972, Jackie Robinson died. The eulogy was delivered by a young minister named Jesse Jackson. He spoke for all black Americans when he said: "When Jackie Robinson took the field something reminded us of our birthright to be free."

About The Author

BARRY DENENBERG is the critically acclaimed author of five other nonfiction books, including *An American Hero: The True Story of Charles A. Lindbergh*, which *Booklist* called, "A superior biography..."; *Voices from Vietnam*, an ALA Best Book for Young Adults and a *Booklist* Editor's Choice Book; and *The True Story of J. Edgar Hoover and the FBI*, of which *VOYA* wrote, "This is an extraordinary book; with it, Denenberg reaches the highest standards of excellence in nonfiction." He has also written one work of historical fiction for Scholastic's *Dear America* series, *When Will This Cruel War Be Over? The Civil War Diary of Emma Simpson*.

Denenberg lives in Bedford, New York, with his wife and their daughter, Emma.

SCHOLASTIC BIOGRAPHY

❑ MP45877-9	Ann M. Martin: The Story of the Author of The Baby-sitters Club	$3.99
❑ MP44767-X	The First Woman Doctor	$3.99
❑ MP43628-7	Freedom Train: The Story of Harriet Tubman	$3.99
❑ MP42402-5	Harry Houdini: Master of Magic	$3.50
❑ MP42404-1	Helen Keller	$3.50
❑ MP44652-5	Helen Keller's Teacher	$3.99
❑ MP44818-8	Invincible Louisa	$3.50
❑ MP42395-9	Jesse Jackson: A Biography	$3.25
❑ MP43503-5	Jim Abbott: Against All Odds	$2.99
❑ MP41159-4	Lost Star: The Story of Amelia Earhart	$3.50
❑ MP44350-X	Louis Braille, The Boy Who Invented Books for the Blind	$3.50
❑ MP48109-6	Malcolm X: By Any Means Necessary	$4.50
❑ MP65174-9	Michael Jordan	$3.50
❑ MP44154-X	Nelson Mandela "No Easy Walk to Freedom"	$3.50
❑ MP42897-7	One More River to Cross: The Stories of Twelve Black Americans	$4.50
❑ MP43052-1	The Secret Soldier: The Story of Deborah Sampson	$2.99
❑ MP44691-6	Sojourner Truth: Ain't I a Woman?	$3.99
❑ MP42560-9	Stealing Home: A Story of Jackie Robinson	$3.99
❑ MP42403-3	The Story of Thomas Alva Edison, Inventor: The Wizard of Menlo Park	$3.50
❑ MP44212-0	Wanted Dead or Alive: The True Story of Harriet Tubman	$3.99
❑ MP42904-3	The Wright Brothers at Kitty Hawk	$3.99

Available wherever you buy books, or use this order form.

Scholastic Inc., P.O. Box 7502, 2931 East McCarty Street, Jefferson City, MO 65102

Please send me the books I have checked above. I am enclosing $_____ (please add $2.00 to cover shipping and handling). Send check or money order — no cash or C.O.D.s please.

Name_____ Birthdate_____

Address_____

City_____ State/Zip _____

Please allow four to six weeks for delivery. Available in the U.S. only. Sorry, mail orders are not available to residents of Canada. Prices subject to change.   BIO997